For Hannah, nurse extraordinaire
—B.H.

For all the healthcare workers
—M.C.

I'm a Virus!

by Bridget Heos
illustrated by Mike Ciccotello

Crown Books for Young Readers
New York

Hi there! I'm Virus!

No, not her. That's my hostess with the mostest. She has the sniffles.

Whee! Off to a new host. I am not alone.
Each virus particle is called a virion. Lots of us fly
in droplets of snot to . . .

. . . your nose!

Zoom in. Closer. That's a nose hair. That's a booger.

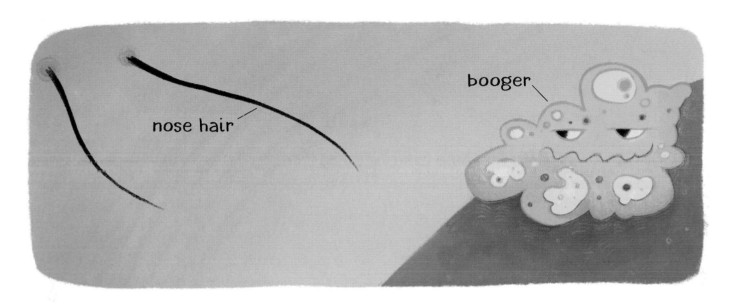

Closer. Closer.

You have trillions of cells.

They are so small they can only be seen under a microscope. But together, they make up your body, from your blood to your bones and even the inside of your nose!

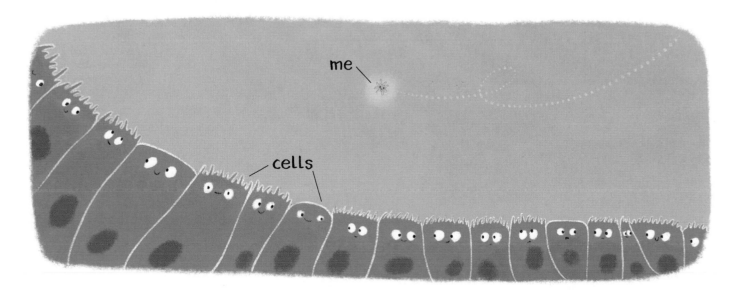

This is Cell. And this is its friend Snot Cell. Snot Cell makes—
you guessed it—snot! Cell pumps that snot away with hairlike
things called cilia.

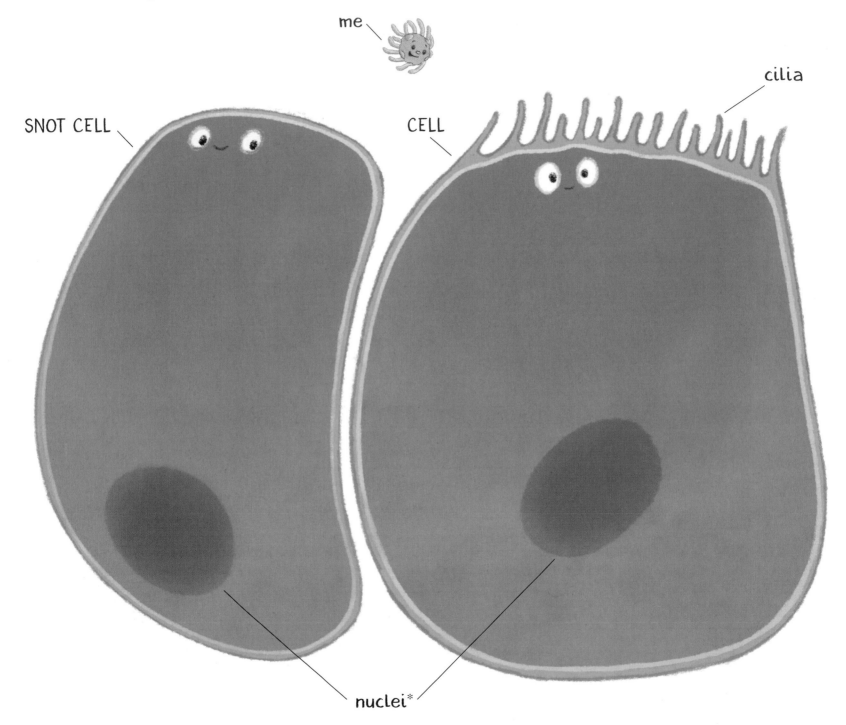

me

cilia

SNOT CELL

CELL

nuclei*

*The parts of cells that tell cells what to do—like make more of me!

Shhhh . . . don't tell Cell, but I am here to attack it. I am a rhinovirus. *Rhino* means "nose." I invade nose cells to cause the common cold.

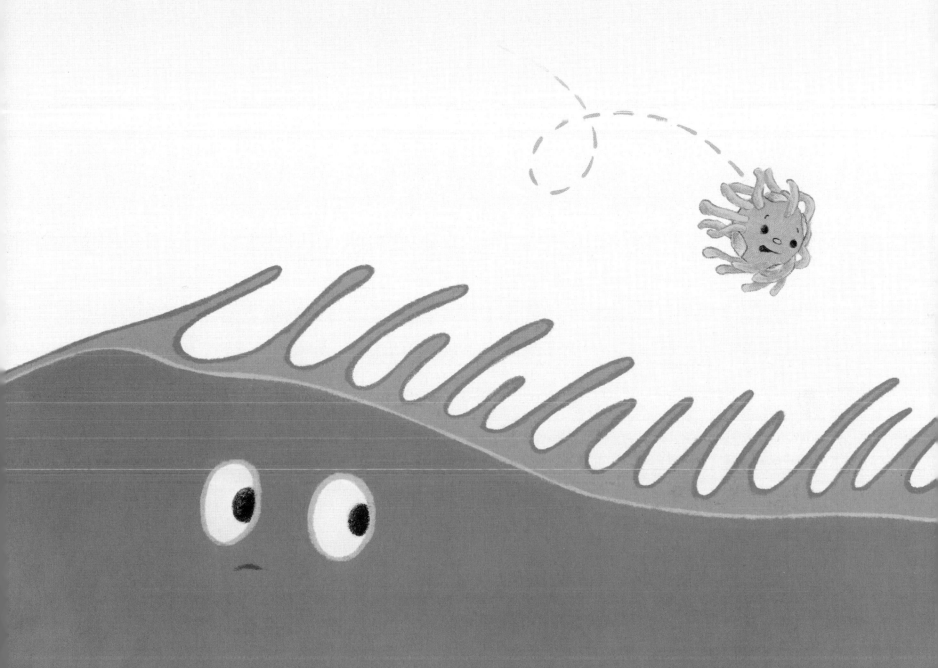

I'm pretty simple, really—a strand of RNA surrounded by a spiky protein shell. My spikes fit perfectly onto Cell's surface. You might say we are a perfect match—like a key in a lock. Cell opens up and lets me in.

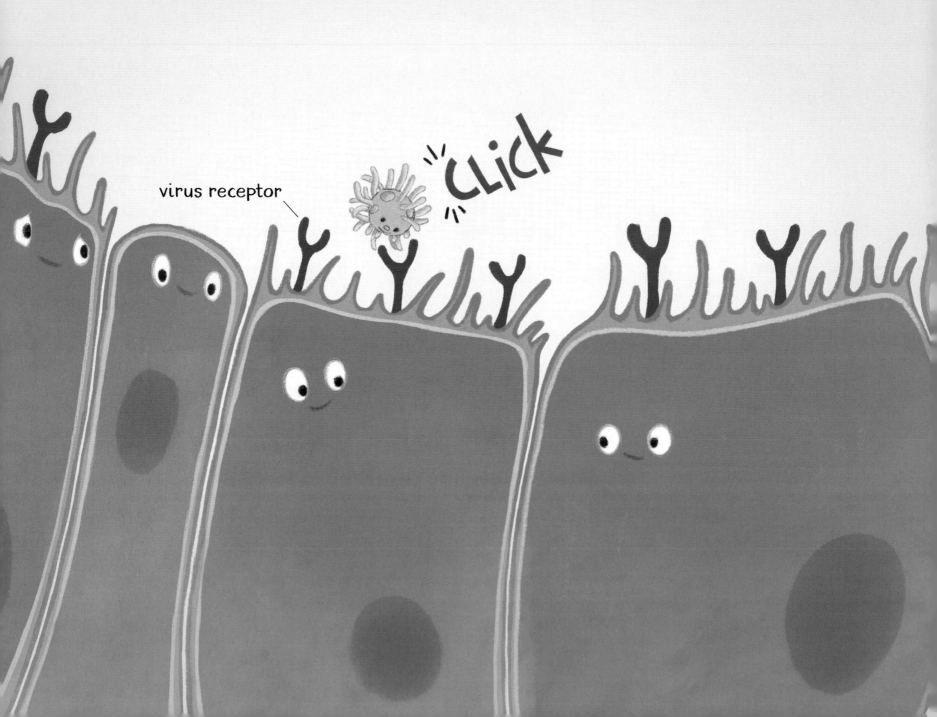

virus receptor

Click

Then I shrug off my spiky jacket so RNA can do its job.
Off it goes to deliver its chemical code message to Cell:

Make more of me. Lots more!

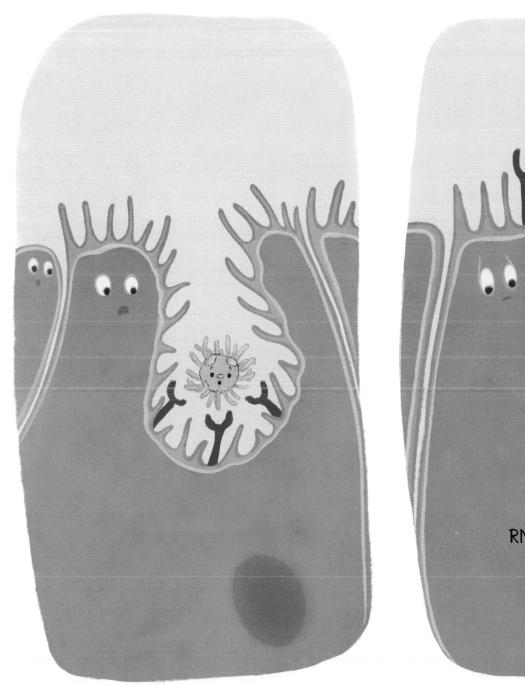
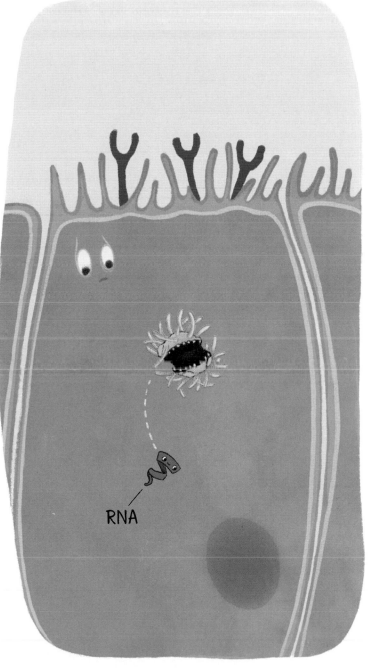

RNA

Uh-oh! It's getting crowded in here.

Pop!

Er, sorry about that, Cell.

Now even more of us can . . .

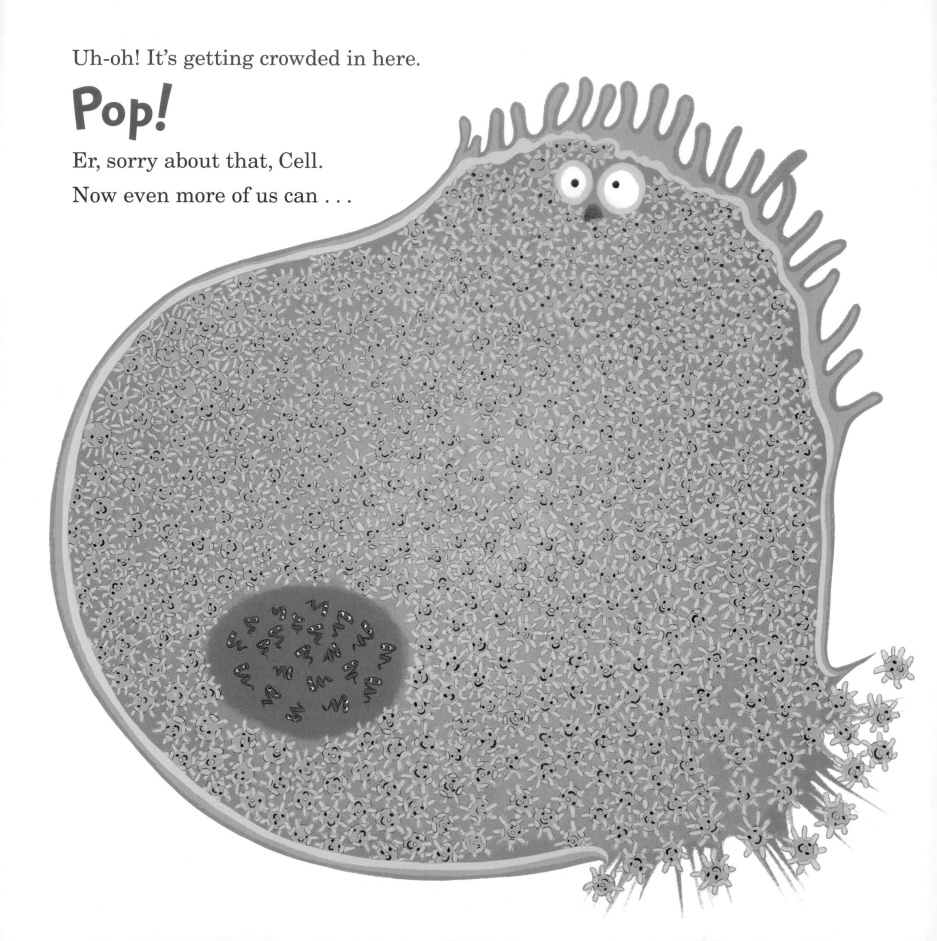

Through all this, you feel fine. Yay! The truth is, I don't want to make you sick. If you are up and about, you can spread me to others!

Meanwhile, my fellow virions invade more and more cells.

Soon our secret plan is not so secret!
An army of white blood cells flows
through your body in blood vessels.

As part of your immune system, some of them release a chemical that causes blood vessels in your nostrils to expand. That gives you a stuffy nose.

The wider blood vessels carry more blood—and bring more white blood cells to the fight. Yikes!

White blood cells bust through the blood vessels to . . .

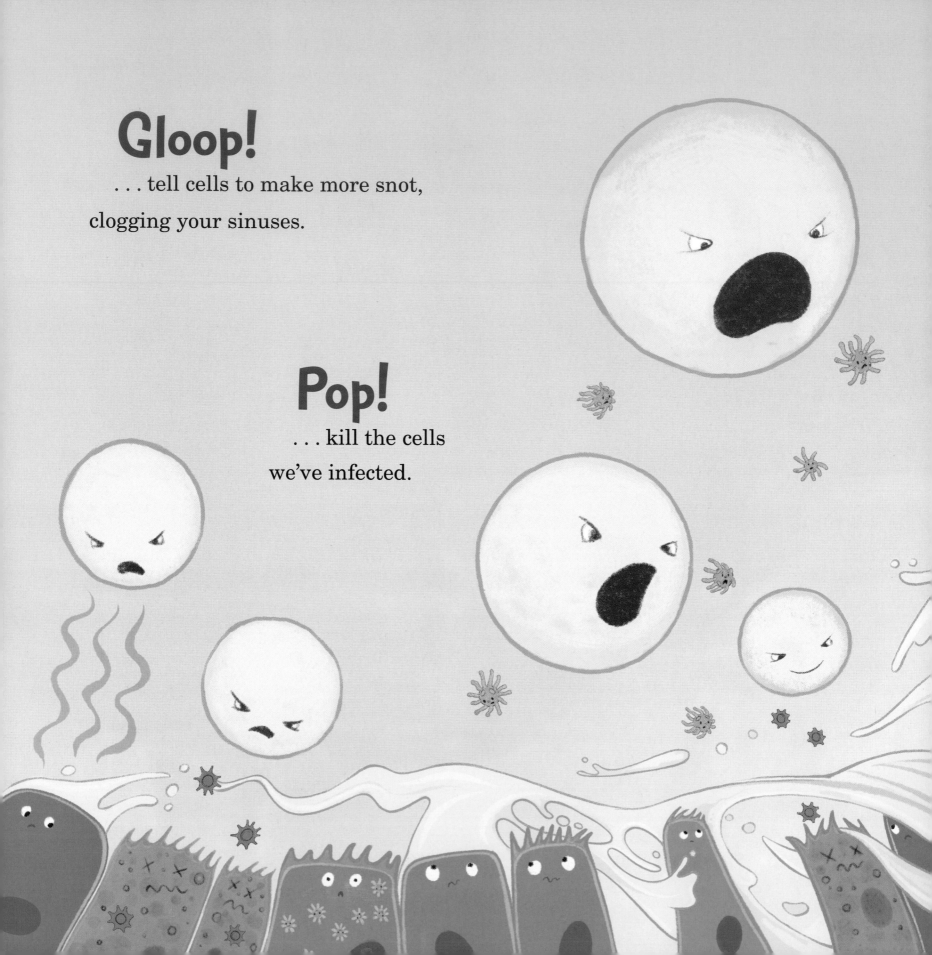

You now have a headache and a runny nose. Don't blame me. . . . That's your white blood cells' fault!

(But if they didn't stop me, I would keep destroying your cells, and that would be my fault.)

By now, you may be feeling too sick to go to school.

Sleep helps your immune system fight me.

Ugh, is that what I think it is?

Soup nourishes your body and gets the mucus flowing again.

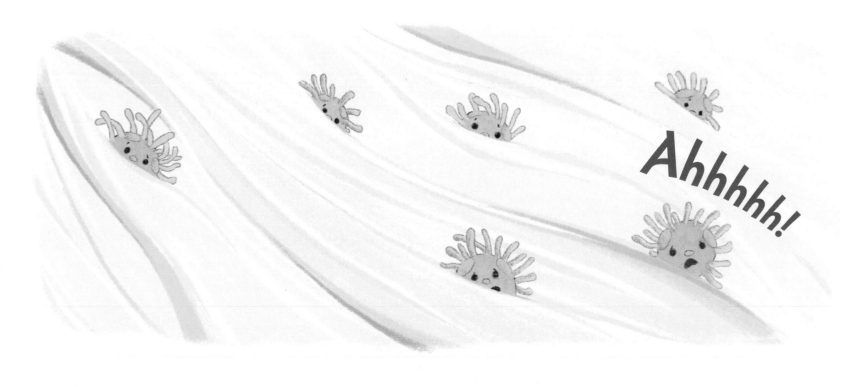

Ahhhhh!

Finally, the white blood cells overrun my defenses.
They've learned how to make antibodies that surround
me so I can no longer attack cells.
    Then the white blood cells devour me faster and faster.
The last of us is gone . . . but not forgotten.

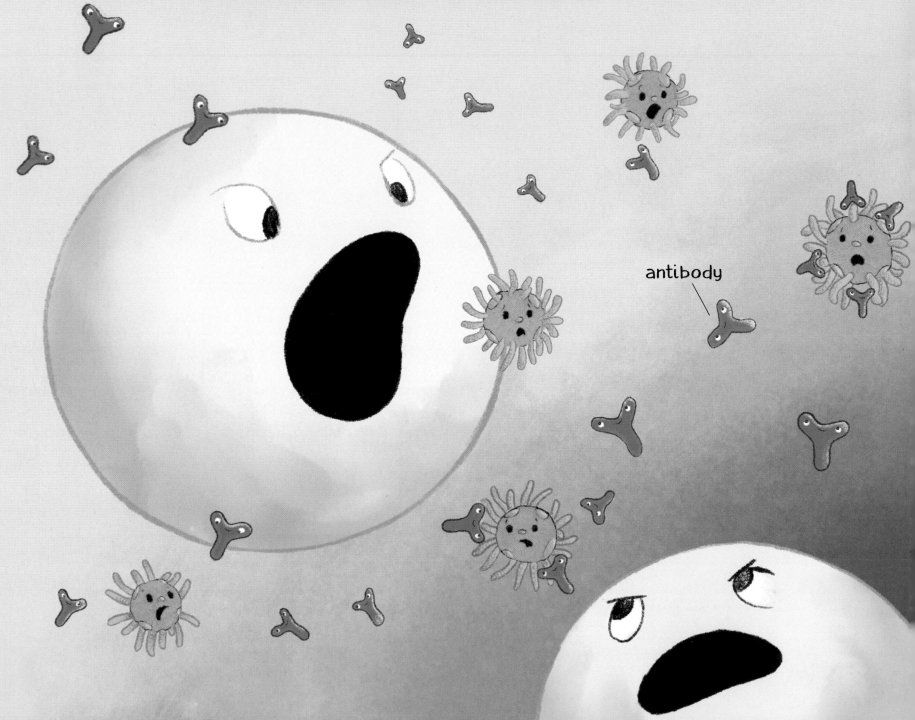

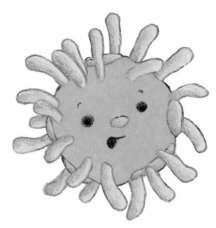

Even though you feel better, your white blood cells keep making antibodies so they can kill me quickly if I attack again.

Enough about me. Let's talk about my fellow viruses.
These viruses used to make children very sick. Now that
can be prevented by vaccines.

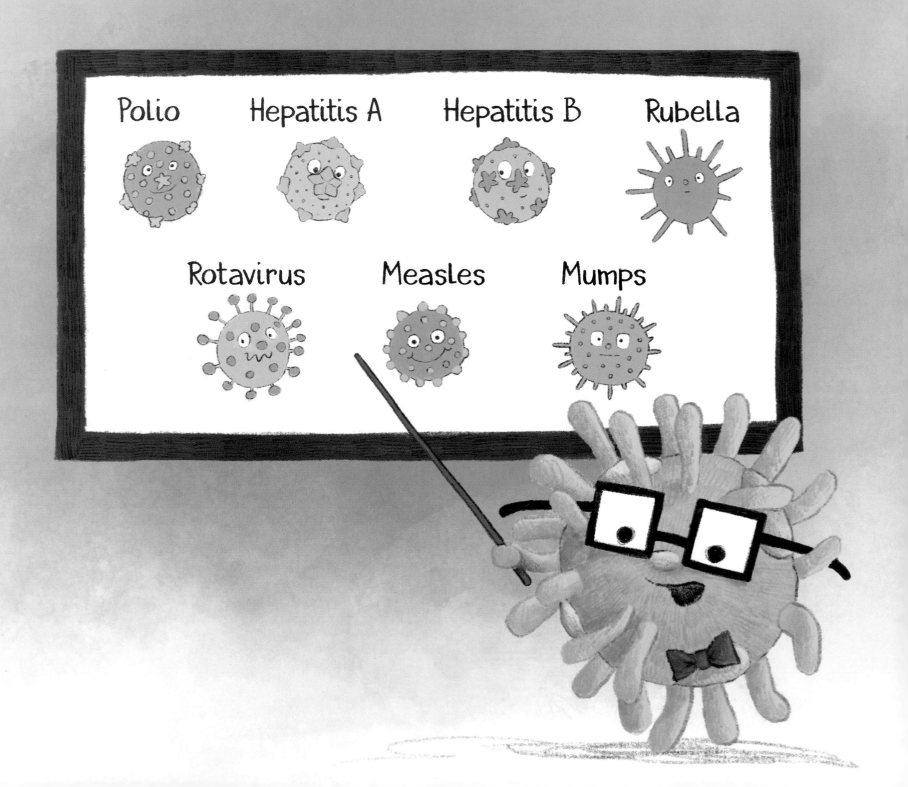

Healthy people are injected with part of the virus or instructions for cells to make part of the virus. Afterward, their white blood cells produce antibodies to be ready if that real virus invades.

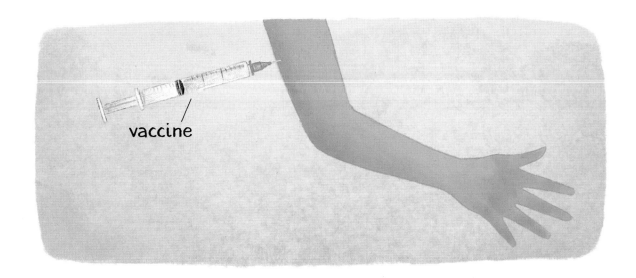

vaccine

Most vaccines can protect you for a lifetime. But some viruses, like the flu, can change so much that your body no longer recognizes it. Then a new vaccine is needed.

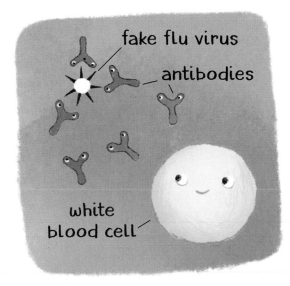

fake flu virus

antibodies

white blood cell

real flu virus

The common cold does not have a vaccine. That's because there are more than one hundred strains of rhinovirus, as well as other viruses, that can cause a cold.

Cough, cough!

I am the new coronavirus, aka COVID-19.

NO ONE has ever seen me before! So I can get EVERYONE sick, and they can infect anyone they cough, sneeze, or breathe on.

This can lead to a pandemic, an outbreak that spreads from country to country.

I'm not just new. I can be dangerous.
I am the perfect match for many cells,
so I can damage much of the body—
from your brain to your lungs to your
toes. The white blood cells fight but
can't keep up! Soon I'm everywhere.
And by the time this host is sick,
I'm off to new hosts, too!

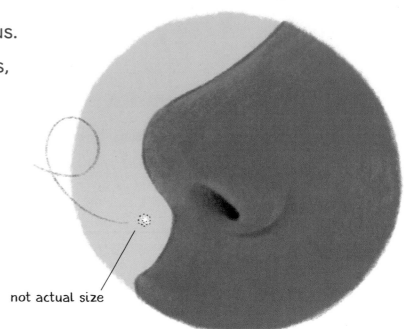

not actual size

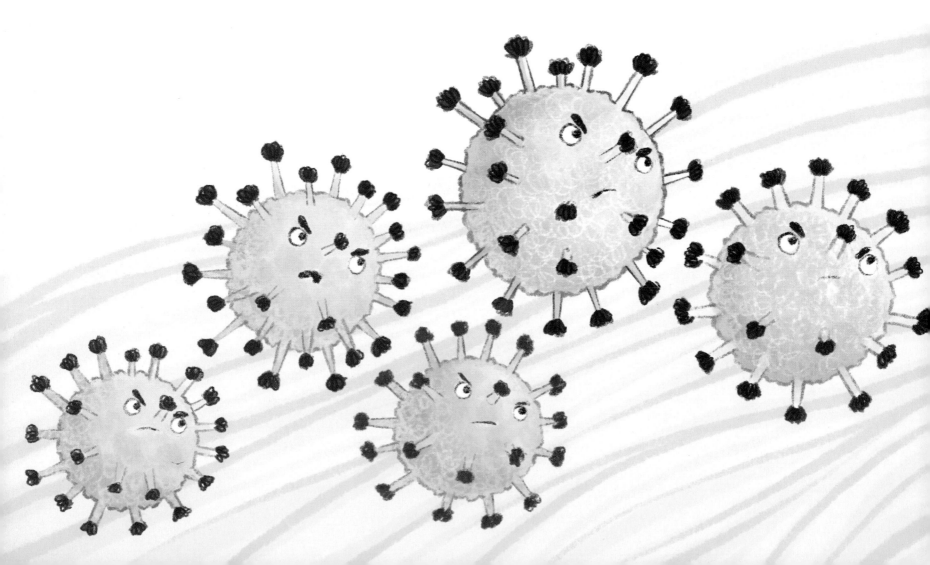

But what is this? It's as if the white blood cells were expecting me.

Sorry, COVID-19. There is a vaccine now. That means you can't go around infecting everyone anymore.

Sigh. You must think all viruses are bad. We're not! Viruses are everywhere. Some of us attack YOUR cells, but others attack bacteria. Bacteria are single-cell organisms that multiply quickly. If we didn't kill some of them, there would be way too many . . . in the soil and the oceans and even inside you!

So good job, us. Next time you sneeze, be sure to cover your mouth, wash your hands, and remember the small but mighty virus!

SMALLPOX: THE BIG IDEA THAT LED TO VACCINES

For thousands of years, smallpox outbreaks ravished people in Europe, Asia, and Africa. The virus caused a rash of pus-filled bumps that eventually scabbed over, along with a host of dangerous symptoms. Three in ten victims died.

People could get smallpox only once. So when epidemics broke out, survivors were already protected. Sadly, Europeans brought smallpox with them to the Americas, exposing indigenous people for the first time. This and other European viruses killed up to 90 percent of the population, tragically changing the course of history for these nations.

Meanwhile, in Asia, doctors had a big idea: to expose healthy people to a small amount of the disease in hopes that they would become mildly ill and then be immune. Using scabs from smallpox sufferers, they either blew the virus into people's noses or scratched it into the skin. The process, known as variolation, was mostly effective but sometimes caused severe smallpox and death.

The practice spread. Then, in 1796, Dr. Edward Jenner discovered that having cowpox also protected people from smallpox. Using this less dangerous disease, he created the first vaccine. Later, a worldwide vaccination effort ended smallpox. Today, many more vaccines prevent deadly diseases.

MEET YOUR BODY'S DEFENDERS!

There are different types of white blood cells with different jobs.

 1. **Mast cells** patrol the body, searching for germs.

 4. **Natural killer cells** destroy cells already infected by the virus.

 2. **Neutrophils** eat one virion each. Then they die.

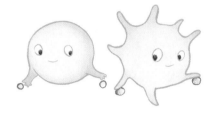 5. **Macrophages** and **dendritic cells** gather information about the germs.

 3. **Macrophages** eat around 100 virions before dying.

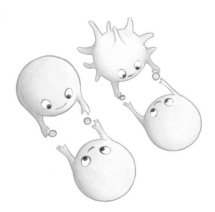 6. They deliver the information to **B cells** and **T cells.**

7. **B cells** make antibodies—Y-shaped chemicals—that surround germs so they can no longer attack cells.

8. When the germ is defeated, **B cells** and **T cells** remember it. If the same germ attacks again, they alert other white blood cells.

9. So next time, all the white blood cells can attack right away!

GLOSSARY

Antibodies—Y-shaped proteins made by white blood cells. When they attach to substances (known as antigens) on the outside of a germ, that germ can no longer attack cells.

Antigens—substances on the surface of germs that are unique to that germ. White blood cells make antibodies that are a perfect fit for antigens.

Bacteria—single-cell microorganisms that live inside humans and in the world around them. Some are helpful to humans and some are harmful.

Blood vessels—the tubes in the body through which blood flows

Cell—the smallest unit of life. Cells join together to make body parts.

Coronavirus—a family of viruses that mainly infects the respiratory system; there are seven coronaviruses that can infect humans, including the new one that causes COVID-19.

Germ (also called a pathogen)—a microorganism, such as a bacterium or virus, that invades the body and causes disease

Nasal cell—a cell that makes up the lining of the nasal cavity

Rhinovirus—a virus that infects the nose and upper respiratory system, causing the common cold

RNA—ribonucleic acid, a single-strand molecule in which chemicals line up to form instructions for cells. In the case of viruses, the instructions are to make more viruses.

Vaccine—a medicine that mimics a germ so that white blood cells are ready to fight back quickly if the germ attacks

Virus—a particle made of DNA or RNA enclosed in a protein shell. Some viruses infect human cells and can be either harmful or helpful.

White blood cells—cells that travel through the blood vessels to attack viruses and other pathogens

FOR FURTHER READING

Ben-Barak, Idan, and Julian Frost. *Do Not Lick This Book.* New York: Roaring Brook Press, 2018.

Davies, Nicola, and Emily Sutton. *Tiny Creatures: The World of Microbes.* Somerville, MA: Candlewick, 2016.

Slade, Suzanne, and Elisa Paganelli. *June Almeida, Virus Detective!* Ann Arbor, MI: Sleeping Bear Press, 2021.

SELECT BIBLIOGRAPHY

"Animation: Developing immunological memory." Wellcome Trust. January 8, 2015. YouTube video, 6:30. Retrieved September 12, 2020. youtube.com/watch?v=SSYOVbEQj_4

Bardi, Jason Socrates. "The Gross Science of a Cough and a Sneeze." *Live Science.* June 14, 2009. Obtained October 12, 2020. livescience.com/3686-gross-science-cough-sneeze.html

"Complement System Made Easy—Immunology—Classical Alternate & Lectin Pathway." MEDSimplified. February 21, 2017. YouTube video, 6:39. Retrieved September 14, 2020. youtube.com/watch?v=d6qFPegEYV0

Cox, Elizabeth. "What Is a Coronavirus?" TED-Ed. May 14, 2020. YouTube video, 5:15. Retrieved September 10, 2020. youtube.com/watch?v=D9tTi-CDjDU

"Diseases You Almost Forgot About (Thanks to Vaccines)." Centers for Disease Control and Prevention. Retrieved September 5, 2020. cdc.gov/vaccines/parents/diseases/forgot-14-diseases.html

Gallagher, James. "Common Cold 'Prefers Cold Noses.'" BBC News. January 6, 2015. Retrieved September 8, 2020. bbc.com/news/health-30685732

Heinze, Susanna. "Immune System." *Science with Susanna.* April 28, 2019. YouTube video, 16:10. Retrieved October 1, 2020. youtube.com/watch?v=QdYuibhnUuE

"Immune System." Microbiology Society. Retrieved September 5, 2020. microbiologysociety.org/why-microbiology-matters/what-is-microbiology/microbes-and-the-human-body/immune-system.html

"Immune System Made Easy: Immunology Innate and Adaptive Immunity Simple Animation." MEDSimplified. March 1, 2020. YouTube video, 25:08. Retrieved September 14, 2020. youtube.com/watch?v=k9QAyP3bYmc

Krulwich, Robert, David Bolinsky, and Jason Orfanon. "Flu Attack! How a Virus Invades Your Body." NPR. October 23, 2009. YouTube video, 3:30. Retrieved September 10, 2020. youtube.com/watch?v=Rpj0emEGShQ

Michos, Erin Donnelly. "Can Coronavirus Cause Heart Damage?" Johns Hopkins Medicine. April 24, 2020. Retrieved November 11, 2020. hopkinsmedicine.org/health/conditions-and-diseases/coronavirus/can-coronavirus-cause-heart-damage

Molnar, Charles, and Jane Gair. "Innate Immune Response." *Concepts of Biology,* 1st Canadian ed. Houston: Rice University, 2013. Retrieved September 15, 2020. opentextbc.ca/biology/chapter/23-1-innate-immune-response/

Oldstone, Michael B. A. *Viruses, Plagues, and History.* New York: Oxford University Press, 2010.

Roossinck, Marilyn J. *Virus: An Illustrated Guide to 101 Incredible Microbes.* Princeton, NJ: Princeton University Press, 2016.

Ryan, Frank. *Virusphere.* London: William Collins, 2019.

Topol, Eric J. "COVID-19 Can Affect the Heart." *Science.* October 23, 2020. Retrieved November 11, 2020. science.sciencemag.org/content/370/6515/408

Wadman, Meredith, Jennifer Couzin-Frankel, Jocelyn Kaiser, and Catherine Matacac. "How Does Coronavirus Kill? Clinicians Trace a Ferocious Rampage Through the Body, from Brain to Toes." *Science.* April 17, 2020. Retrieved November 11, 2020. sciencemag.org/news/2020/04/how-does-coronavirus-kill-clinicians-trace-ferocious-rampage-through-body-brain-toes